Imagined Futures

Exploring Latino Narratives Through Design Fiction

A Journey into Speculative Storytelling and Cultural Innovation

Alessio rocchI

Table of Contents

Introduction: Reimagining the Future Through Culture and Design

This introduction sets the stage for exploring how speculative storytelling rooted in Latino culture intersects with design fiction to create thought-provoking narratives. It explains the significance of both topics and outlines the book's unique approach to envisioning possible futures.

Chapter 1: Understanding Speculative Storytelling

This chapter provides an overview of speculative fiction, tracing its history and core elements. It highlights how this genre imagines alternative realities and explores themes of science, technology, and societal change.

Chapter 2: The Rich Tapestry of Latino Narratives

A deep dive into the diverse stories, folklore, and cultural elements that define Latino literature. This chapter introduces key themes such as resilience, migration, identity, and community that form the foundation of Latino speculative storytelling.

Chapter 3: What is Design Fiction?

An accessible explanation of design fiction, its origins, and how it uses speculative artifacts to provoke thought and inspire new ideas. Real-world examples illustrate how this method shapes conversations about the future.

Chapter 4: Where Culture Meets Speculation

This chapter examines how blending Latino cultural elements with speculative fiction creates powerful narratives. It discusses the role of tradition and innovation in imagining alternative futures.

Chapter 5: Building Futures with Design Fiction

Practical insights into using design fiction to construct stories and scenarios. Readers learn techniques for designing speculative artifacts, such as fictional products or systems, that reflect cultural and societal themes.

Chapter 6: Case Studies in Latino Design Fiction

A showcase of original examples and case studies where Latino narratives are reimagined through the lens of design fiction. These scenarios explore themes like migration in futuristic worlds, climate adaptation, and redefined community structures.

Chapter 7: Writing Your Own Speculative Stories

A hands-on guide to crafting speculative fiction inspired by Latino culture. This chapter provides tips on blending cultural authenticity with imaginative storytelling and offers exercises to develop unique story ideas.

Chapter 8: Designing Fictional Futures

This chapter builds on the previous one, focusing on how to incorporate design fiction principles into storytelling. It includes examples of speculative designs and how they enhance narratives.

Chapter 9: The Impact of Speculative Narratives

An exploration of the transformative power of speculative storytelling and design fiction in shaping perceptions, sparking innovation, and fostering cultural appreciation.

Chapter 10: Looking Ahead—The Future of Storytelling and Design

The final chapter envisions the potential evolution of speculative storytelling and design fiction, highlighting opportunities for readers to contribute their voices to this growing field.

Appendices

Introduction

Reimagining the Future Through Culture and Design

The human imagination is an extraordinary force—a boundless resource that transcends limitations of time, space, and circumstance. From the earliest cave paintings to contemporary speculative fiction, humans have used storytelling to explore the unknown and project their hopes, fears, and dreams onto the canvas of the future. At the heart of this creative endeavor lies an intricate relationship between culture and imagination, a dynamic interplay that shapes and reshapes the stories we tell about who we are and who we might become.

This book, *Imagined Futures: Exploring Latino Narratives Through Design Fiction*, delves into an exciting confluence of two powerful frameworks: speculative storytelling rooted in Latino cultural narratives and the emerging discipline of design fiction. Each of these domains is compelling on its own, but when fused, they create a fertile ground for reimagining the future in ways that are both deeply personal and universally resonant.

The Power of Speculative Storytelling

Speculative fiction is often seen as a genre of "what ifs," offering hypothetical scenarios that challenge conventional thinking. It includes science fiction, fantasy, alternate history, and other subgenres that question the boundaries of reality. While speculative fiction is sometimes dismissed as escapist or purely fantastical, its power lies in its ability to illuminate truths about the human condition and inspire new ways of thinking about the world.

Consider the enduring appeal of classics like *1984* or *The Handmaid's Tale*, which use speculative frameworks to critique societal norms and explore dystopian futures. These narratives resonate because they are rooted in current realities, extrapolated to extremes. They challenge readers to reflect on their own societies and imagine the consequences of particular paths. In this sense, speculative fiction serves as both a mirror and a crystal ball.

Latino speculative storytelling takes this genre to new heights, blending rich cultural traditions with imaginative narratives. Drawing on a heritage of folklore, mythology, and oral storytelling, Latino writers infuse speculative fiction with themes of identity, resilience, and community. The stories they tell are grounded in cultural specificity, yet they transcend boundaries, offering universal insights into the complexities of human experience.

Latino Narratives: A Treasure Trove of Cultural Richness

The Latino cultural experience is as diverse as the people who identify with it. Spanning countries, languages, and histories, Latino narratives are imbued with a sense of movement and transformation. Themes of migration, adaptation, and cultural hybridity are central to these stories, reflecting the lived realities of many Latino individuals and communities.

Folklore plays a significant role in shaping Latino narratives, offering a repository of symbols and archetypes that continue to inspire contemporary storytelling. Figures like *La Llorona*, the weeping woman of Mexican legend, or *El Cucuy*, the bogeyman of many Latin American cultures, appear in tales that serve both as cautionary fables and as windows into collective fears and desires. These stories are not static relics of the past but living traditions that evolve over time, incorporating new elements and interpretations.

The Latino experience is also marked by resilience—a quality born of enduring adversity and finding strength in community. This resilience manifests in speculative narratives as characters who defy odds, rebuild worlds, and imagine futures where justice and equity prevail. By drawing on their cultural heritage, Latino writers offer perspectives that are at once deeply personal and broadly resonant, inviting readers to see the world through new eyes.

Introducing Design Fiction: The Art of Imagining Futures

While speculative storytelling focuses on narratives, design fiction adds a tangible dimension to the act of imagining the future. Originating as a practice within the design community, design fiction involves creating artifacts, scenarios, or systems that represent possible futures. These artifacts—whether they take the form of a fictional product, a prototype, or a speculative advertisement—are designed not to predict the future but to provoke thought and spark dialogue.

Design fiction operates at the intersection of imagination and pragmatism. Unlike traditional design, which seeks to solve current problems, design fiction explores what might be possible, encouraging people to think critically about potential outcomes. By creating a "future-to-present" feedback loop, design fiction helps individuals and organizations anticipate challenges, identify opportunities, and make informed decisions about the paths they choose to pursue.

Consider, for example, the concept of a fictional app that calculates the carbon footprint of daily activities. While such an app may not yet exist, its creation as a design fiction artifact invites questions about environmental responsibility, personal accountability, and the role of technology in shaping behavior. These questions, in turn, can influence real-world innovation and policy-making.

The Intersection of Culture and Design

What happens when the rich tapestry of Latino culture intersects with the speculative possibilities of design fiction? The result is a creative synergy that redefines how we think about the future. Latino design fiction combines cultural authenticity with imaginative exploration, offering visions of the future that are deeply rooted in heritage yet boldly innovative.

One of the most exciting aspects of this fusion is its ability to challenge dominant narratives about the future. Too often, depictions of the future are homogenized, reflecting the perspectives of a narrow demographic. Latino design fiction disrupts this pattern by introducing diverse voices and perspectives, ensuring that the imagined futures are as varied and multifaceted as the people who inhabit them.

For example, a Latino design fiction project might envision a future where migration is celebrated as a source of strength and innovation, rather than stigmatized as a challenge to be managed. It might imagine a world where traditional practices of communal living are integrated into urban planning, creating cities that prioritize connection and sustainability. By blending cultural elements with speculative design, these projects offer fresh perspectives on pressing global issues.

Stories as Blueprints for Change

At its core, Latino design fiction is about storytelling. The artifacts and scenarios created through this practice are not ends in themselves but means of conveying ideas and sparking conversation. They serve as blueprints for change, offering visions of what could be and inviting others to join in the act of creation.

Storytelling has always been a powerful tool for change. It allows us to articulate our values, share our experiences, and build empathy across differences. In the context of design fiction, storytelling becomes a way of testing ideas, exploring possibilities, and imagining new ways of being. When infused with the richness of Latino culture, these stories become even more potent, offering a lens through which to examine the intersections of identity, innovation, and aspiration.

The Role of the Reader in Imagined Futures

While this book offers a roadmap for exploring Latino narratives through design fiction, it is not a prescriptive guide. Instead, it is an invitation—a call to engage with the ideas presented here and to contribute to the ongoing dialogue about the future. The reader's role is not passive but active, as a co-creator of the stories and visions that will shape tomorrow.

In reading this book, you will encounter a diverse array of perspectives, techniques, and examples. Some may resonate deeply with your own experiences, while others may challenge you to think differently. Both responses are valuable, for they are the hallmarks of engagement and growth. As you navigate these pages, consider how the concepts presented here might inform your own storytelling, whether as a writer, a designer, or simply a dreamer of what might be.

This journey into imagined futures is not just about exploring possibilities—it is about creating them. By blending the richness of Latino cultural narratives with the visionary potential of design fiction, we can reimagine the world not as it is but as it could be, crafting a future that is as inclusive, diverse, and inspiring as the stories that shape it.

Chapter 1

Understanding Speculative Storytelling

Speculative storytelling is not just a genre—it is a mode of human expression that allows us to question, explore, and reimagine our reality. From ancient myths to contemporary science fiction, speculative storytelling provides the framework to imagine alternate possibilities, pose "what if" scenarios, and probe the consequences of change. In this chapter, we will delve deeply into the roots, evolution, and potential of speculative storytelling, examining how it has shaped and been shaped by culture, technology, and imagination.

The Origins of Speculative Storytelling: Myths, Legends, and Folklore

Speculative storytelling has its origins in the earliest human attempts to understand the world. Myths and legends, the precursors to modern speculative fiction, were humanity's first speculative narratives. These stories did more than entertain—they provided frameworks for explaining the unexplainable, codifying moral codes, and offering visions of creation and destruction.

In nearly every culture, myths and legends contain elements of speculation. They imagine the origins of life, the workings of natural phenomena, and the nature of gods and spirits. For example, the ancient Greek myth of Prometheus stealing fire from the gods is a speculative tale about technology, creativity, and rebellion. Similarly, the Mayan *Popol Vuh* explores the creation of humanity through a lens of divine experimentation and failure, reflecting deep cultural understandings of identity and purpose.

These early speculative narratives share many characteristics with modern science fiction and fantasy. They often depict worlds governed by rules different from our own, populated by beings with extraordinary powers, and shaped by forces beyond human comprehension. In this way, myths and legends laid the groundwork for the speculative genres we know today.

Speculative Storytelling in Literature: From Gothic Horror to Science Fiction

As societies evolved, so did their speculative narratives. The rise of written literature allowed for more complex and nuanced explorations of speculative themes. Gothic horror, for instance, emerged in the 18th century as a way to probe humanity's deepest fears—fear of the unknown, fear of the supernatural, and fear of progress. Mary Shelley's *Frankenstein* is a prime example, blending elements of horror and science fiction to question the ethics of scientific discovery and the limits of human ambition.

In the 19th and 20th centuries, speculative storytelling expanded into distinct genres such as science fiction, fantasy, and dystopian literature. Jules Verne and H.G. Wells are often credited as pioneers of science fiction, imagining futuristic technologies and exploring their potential impacts on society. Verne's *20,000 Leagues Under the Sea* speculated about underwater exploration long before submarines became a reality, while Wells' *The War of the Worlds* envisioned interplanetary conflict and the existential threat of extraterrestrial life.

Fantasy also flourished during this period, drawing heavily from mythology and folklore but creating new worlds with their own internal logic. J.R.R. Tolkien's *The Lord of the Rings* epitomized this trend, offering an epic narrative that combined the richness of ancient myths with a modern sensibility.

Dystopian literature, another branch of speculative storytelling, emerged as a response to political and social upheaval. Works like George Orwell's *1984* and Aldous Huxley's *Brave New World* used speculative scenarios to critique totalitarianism, consumerism, and technological overreach. These stories did not merely predict the future—they served as warnings, urging readers to reflect on the trajectories of their societies.

The Mechanics of Speculative Storytelling

At its core, speculative storytelling is about asking questions and imagining answers. It operates on the principle of extrapolation, taking a current trend, technology, or cultural phenomenon and extending it into the future or reimagining it in a different context. This process often involves three key elements:

1. **World-Building**

   World-building is the foundation of speculative storytelling. It involves creating a setting with its own rules, histories, and logic. In speculative fiction, the world is as much a character as the protagonists themselves, influencing the story's events and themes. For example, in Margaret Atwood's *The Handmaid's Tale*, the dystopian society of Gilead is meticulously constructed, with detailed hierarchies, rituals, and laws that reflect the story's critique of patriarchy and authoritarianism.

2. **Speculation**

   The speculative element is what sets these stories apart from other forms of fiction. It involves imagining something that does not exist in our reality—whether it's advanced technology, magical powers, or alternate histories. The speculative element often serves as a lens through which the author examines real-world issues. For instance, Octavia Butler's *Parable of the Sower* uses the backdrop of a climate-ravaged America to explore themes of resilience, community, and belief.

3. **Narrative**

   Despite its imaginative settings and speculative elements, the success of speculative storytelling ultimately hinges on its narrative. Readers connect with stories through characters, conflicts, and resolutions. Even the most fantastical worlds must be grounded in human (or relatable) experiences to resonate with audiences. Speculative narratives thrive on the tension between the familiar and the unfamiliar, allowing readers to see their own world in a new light.

Cultural Influences on Speculative Storytelling

Speculative storytelling is deeply influenced by the cultural context in which it is created. Stories reflect the fears, hopes, and values of their societies, often addressing pressing issues through a speculative lens. For example, Cold War-era science fiction frequently dealt with themes of nuclear annihilation and alien invasion, reflecting anxieties about geopolitical tensions and technological advancement.

Latino speculative storytelling, the focus of this book, offers a particularly rich tapestry of cultural influences. It draws on the myths, legends, and historical experiences of Latino communities, weaving them into narratives that explore identity, resilience, and transformation. Works like Silvia Moreno-Garcia's *Mexican Gothic* or Gabriel García Márquez's *One Hundred Years of Solitude* exemplify this blend of cultural authenticity and speculative imagination.

Latino speculative stories often challenge dominant narratives, offering alternative perspectives on history, society, and the future. They may reimagine historical events from the viewpoint of marginalized communities, explore the interplay between tradition and modernity, or envision futures where cultural hybridity is a source of strength.

Speculative Storytelling Across Media

While literature has long been the primary medium for speculative storytelling, other forms of media have embraced and expanded its possibilities. Film, television, video games, and graphic novels offer new ways to engage with speculative narratives, each with its own strengths and limitations.

- **Film and Television**
  Visual storytelling mediums like film and television bring

speculative worlds to life with unparalleled immediacy. From the sprawling universes of *Star Wars* to the dystopian landscapes of *Black Mirror*, these stories use visual and auditory elements to immerse audiences in their imagined realities. Latino filmmakers and creators are increasingly contributing to this space, with projects like Guillermo del Toro's *The Shape of Water* and Disney's *Encanto* showcasing the richness of Latino culture through speculative narratives.

- **Video Games**

  Video games offer a unique form of speculative storytelling by allowing players to actively participate in the narrative. Games like *Cyberpunk 2077* or *Horizon Zero Dawn* create immersive speculative worlds where players can explore, make choices, and experience the consequences of their actions. These interactive experiences deepen the engagement with speculative themes, making players co-creators of the story.

- **Graphic Novels and Comics**

  Graphic novels and comics combine visual artistry with storytelling, making them a powerful medium for speculative fiction. Works like *Watchmen* or *La Borinqueña* use the interplay of text and imagery to explore complex themes and create vivid speculative worlds.

Speculative Storytelling as a Tool for Change

Speculative storytelling is more than entertainment—it is a tool for change. By imagining alternate realities, it allows us to question the status quo, explore the consequences of our actions, and envision better futures. In this sense, speculative stories are not just mirrors of our world—they are blueprints for what could be.

For marginalized communities, speculative storytelling can be particularly empowering. It provides a platform to challenge stereotypes, reclaim narratives, and assert the value of diverse perspectives. Latino speculative storytelling, for instance, offers a space to celebrate cultural heritage, critique systemic injustices, and imagine futures where inclusion and equity prevail.

As we explore the intersection of speculative storytelling and design fiction in this book, it is essential to understand the transformative potential of these narratives. They are not just flights of fancy—they are acts of creation, reflection, and resistance. By engaging with speculative storytelling, we not only entertain ourselves but also equip ourselves with the tools to navigate and shape the future.

Chapter 2

The Rich Tapestry of Latino Narratives

Latino narratives are a mosaic of stories, woven together by threads of history, culture, language, and resilience. They transcend borders, reflecting the experiences of diverse communities from Latin America and the Caribbean while intertwining with the complexities of life in the United States. Rich with oral traditions, folklore, and a profound sense of place, these narratives offer insights into identity, survival, and transformation. In this chapter, we will explore the roots of Latino storytelling, its defining characteristics, and its enduring impact on contemporary literature and speculative fiction.

The Historical Roots of Latino Storytelling

Latino storytelling is deeply rooted in the histories of Latin America and the Caribbean, shaped by the intersections of indigenous traditions, European colonialism, and African cultural influences. The pre-Columbian civilizations of the Americas, including the Aztecs, Maya, and Inca, maintained robust oral storytelling traditions that conveyed their cosmologies, histories, and moral teachings.

For example, the Mayan *Popol Vuh*, often referred to as the "Mayan Bible," recounts the creation of the world and the adventures of heroic twin gods. It is an epic of survival, sacrifice, and the interplay between the divine and the mortal—a testament to the rich narrative traditions that existed long before European colonization.

The arrival of Spanish and Portuguese colonizers brought dramatic changes to the region's storytelling traditions. Colonial powers imposed their languages, religions, and cultural norms on indigenous populations, often erasing or suppressing local traditions. However, storytelling proved resilient, adapting to new realities. Indigenous tales absorbed Christian elements, while African traditions introduced by enslaved people blended with existing folklore. The resulting narratives reflect a complex cultural hybridity, rich in symbolism and meaning.

The Role of Oral Traditions

Oral storytelling remains a cornerstone of Latino culture. Before literacy became widespread, stories were shared around fires, in communal gatherings, and through songs. Oral traditions served multiple purposes: preserving history, teaching moral lessons, and fostering a sense of community.

In many rural Latin American communities, tales of *El Sombrerón*, *La Llorona*, and *El Cucuy* were passed down through generations, often with slight variations to reflect local contexts. These stories not only entertained but also conveyed warnings and cultural values. *La Llorona*, for instance, is a ghostly figure who mourns her drowned children and serves as a cautionary tale about motherhood, morality, and consequence.

Oral storytelling also provided a means of resistance. During periods of colonization, slavery, and dictatorship, storytelling became a subversive act, a way to preserve cultural identity and critique oppression. Songs like corridos (Mexican ballads) and décimas (a form of poetry) often carried veiled messages of resistance, chronicling the struggles of marginalized communities.

Themes in Latino Narratives

Latino narratives are distinguished by recurring themes that reflect the experiences and values of their communities. While these themes are diverse, several stand out for their prominence and resonance.

1. **Migration and Diaspora**

   The theme of migration is central to many Latino narratives, reflecting both historical and contemporary realities. From the forced migrations of the transatlantic slave trade to the voluntary migrations of individuals seeking economic opportunities, the movement of people has shaped the Latino experience. Stories of migration often explore the tension between longing for the homeland and adapting to new environments, as well as the struggles of maintaining cultural identity in foreign lands.

   In Sandra Cisneros' *The House on Mango Street*, the protagonist, Esperanza, navigates the complexities of growing up in a Chicano neighborhood in Chicago, dreaming of a life beyond its confines while grappling with the weight of her cultural heritage. Such narratives resonate deeply with readers who have experienced displacement, whether physical or emotional.

2. **Identity and Hybridity**

Latino narratives frequently explore the complexities of identity, particularly the experience of living between cultures. This hybridity manifests in language, food, music, and traditions, often leading to a sense of belonging everywhere and nowhere at once. Junot Díaz's *The Brief Wondrous Life of Oscar Wao* captures this duality, telling the story of a Dominican-American family straddling two worlds. The novel seamlessly weaves English, Spanish, and Dominican slang, reflecting the linguistic hybridity of many Latino communities and emphasizing the layered nature of identity.

3. **Community and Resilience**

The importance of family and community is a hallmark of Latino storytelling. Narratives often depict extended family networks, close-knit neighborhoods, and communal efforts to overcome adversity. These stories celebrate the strength found in unity, portraying resilience as both an individual and collective quality. Esmeralda Santiago's memoir *When I Was Puerto Rican* highlights the challenges and triumphs of growing up in a Puerto Rican family that immigrates to the mainland United States. Her story emphasizes the sacrifices and support systems that sustain families through difficult transitions.

4. **Faith and Spirituality**

Religion and spirituality are deeply ingrained in many Latino narratives. While Catholicism is the dominant faith, it often intertwines with indigenous beliefs and practices, creating a syncretic spirituality that is uniquely Latin American. Stories frequently incorporate themes of faith, miracles, and the supernatural, blending the sacred with the everyday.

Gabriel García Márquez's *One Hundred Years of Solitude* exemplifies this fusion, portraying a world where the miraculous is as ordinary as the mundane. The novel's magical realism captures the interplay between faith, folklore, and the human experience.

5. Social Justice and Resistance

Latino storytelling often addresses issues of social justice, highlighting the struggles of marginalized communities. These narratives critique systemic inequities, from colonization and slavery to contemporary issues such as immigration policies and racial discrimination.

In Luis Alberto Urrea's *The Devil's Highway*, the author recounts the harrowing journey of 26 Mexican migrants attempting to cross the U.S.-Mexico border. The book combines journalism and narrative to shed light on the human cost of border policies, challenging readers to confront the realities of migration.

The Influence of Folklore on Contemporary Narratives

Latino folklore continues to inspire contemporary storytelling, particularly in the realm of speculative fiction. Figures like *La Llorona* and *El Chupacabra* appear not only in traditional tales but also in modern novels, films, and graphic novels, reimagined for new audiences.

For example, Silvia Moreno-Garcia's *Mexican Gothic* draws on Mexican folklore and Gothic horror to tell a chilling story of inheritance and identity. The novel reclaims the Gothic tradition, infusing it with a distinctly Mexican sensibility and challenging colonial narratives.

Folklore also provides a lens through which to explore contemporary issues. In Carmen Maria Machado's *Her Body and Other Parties*, elements of folklore and fairy tales are woven into feminist narratives that examine gender, sexuality, and power. This blending of the traditional and the modern exemplifies the adaptability and enduring relevance of Latino folklore.

Latino Narratives in Speculative Fiction

The speculative fiction genre offers a particularly fertile ground for Latino storytelling, allowing writers to imagine alternative realities that challenge existing power structures and celebrate cultural heritage. Latino speculative fiction often combines elements of science fiction, fantasy, and magical realism, creating narratives that are both deeply rooted in tradition and boldly innovative.

For instance, in *Gods of Jade and Shadow*, Silvia Moreno-Garcia reimagines the Mayan underworld as the backdrop for a fantastical quest. The novel blends mythology, history, and fantasy, creating a story that is uniquely Mexican yet universally resonant.

Latino speculative fiction also frequently addresses themes of migration and hybridity through futuristic lenses. In *Borderline*, Mishell Baker explores issues of disability, identity, and belonging in a speculative world where borders—both physical and metaphysical—are fluid and contested.

The Global Reach of Latino Narratives

While rooted in specific cultural contexts, Latino narratives have a global appeal. Their themes of migration, identity, and resilience resonate with readers from diverse backgrounds, fostering empathy and understanding. Latino writers have received international acclaim, from Gabriel García Márquez's Nobel Prize to the global popularity of authors like Isabel Allende and Julia Alvarez.

In the United States, the influence of Latino narratives is growing, reflecting the increasing prominence of the Latino population. Books like *The Poet X* by Elizabeth Acevedo and *Clap When You Land* capture the experiences of young Latinos in the U.S., addressing universal themes of family, loss, and self-discovery while highlighting the richness of Afro-Latino culture.

Latino narratives are also finding new audiences through translation, film adaptations, and digital platforms. Stories that were once confined to specific regions or languages are now accessible to readers around the world, amplifying the voices of Latino writers and broadening the impact of their work.

Through their richness and diversity, Latino narratives offer a window into the complexities of culture, identity, and the human condition. These stories, steeped in history and tradition yet ever-evolving, challenge us to see the world through new eyes and imagine futures shaped by resilience, creativity, and hope.

Chapter 3

What is Design Fiction?

The concept of design fiction is a relatively new yet profoundly transformative approach to imagining the future. It sits at the intersection of speculative storytelling, critical design, and practical innovation, offering a unique lens through which we can explore possibilities, challenge assumptions, and rethink our relationships with technology, culture, and society. In this chapter, we will delve deeply into the origins, principles, applications, and potential of design fiction, uncovering how it reshapes the way we think about the future and our place within it.

Defining Design Fiction

Design fiction is a practice that uses speculative scenarios, artifacts, and narratives to explore possible futures. Unlike science fiction, which primarily exists to entertain or provoke thought, design fiction is inherently practical. It bridges imagination and reality, serving as a tool for research, innovation, and critical reflection.

At its core, design fiction asks a simple but profound question: *What if?*

- What if technology advanced in unexpected ways?
- What if societal norms shifted radically?

- What if we could redesign the world around us?

By imagining these "what if" scenarios, design fiction creates spaces for discussion, experimentation, and understanding. It goes beyond merely describing potential futures; it immerses people in them, offering tangible glimpses of alternative realities through designed artifacts and experiences.

The Origins of Design Fiction

The term "design fiction" was popularized by Julian Bleecker, a technologist and researcher at the Near Future Laboratory. In his seminal 2009 essay, *Design Fiction: A Short Essay on Design, Science, Fact and Fiction*, Bleecker articulated a vision of design fiction as a means of bridging speculative storytelling and design practice. He argued that by creating fictional artifacts—such as speculative technologies or products—we could better understand the implications of these innovations before they become reality.

However, the roots of design fiction can be traced back even further. Visionary thinkers like Buckminster Fuller and futurists of the 20th century often used speculative designs to provoke thought and challenge conventional wisdom. Fuller's geodesic domes and "Dymaxion" designs were speculative yet grounded in practical application, embodying principles that would later inform design fiction.

Science fiction, too, has long played a role in shaping design fiction's principles. Films like *Blade Runner* and *Minority Report* not only entertained audiences but also inspired real-world innovations, such as voice-activated technology and gesture-based interfaces. The difference between traditional science fiction and design fiction lies in its focus: while science fiction tells stories about the future, design fiction builds artifacts and scenarios that let us *experience* the future.

Key Principles of Design Fiction

Design fiction operates on several guiding principles that differentiate it from other forms of speculative thinking. These principles provide a framework for creating meaningful and thought-provoking futures.

1. **Speculative Yet Plausible**

   Design fiction thrives in the gray area between imagination and reality. Its scenarios are speculative but rooted in plausibility, making them relatable and engaging. A design fiction artifact might envision a self-driving car that doubles as a mobile office—not far-fetched, but layered with implications for work-life balance, privacy, and urban planning.

2. **World-Building Through Artifacts**

   Rather than presenting abstract ideas, design fiction brings them to life through physical or digital artifacts. These could include prototypes, speculative advertisements, user manuals, or even fictional news articles. Each artifact acts as a touchpoint, immersing audiences in the imagined world and making the abstract tangible.

3. **Provocation, Not Prediction**

    Design fiction is not about predicting the future but about
    provoking thought. Its goal is to challenge assumptions, spark
    dialogue, and encourage critical thinking about possible futures.
    For example, a speculative scenario about a future where
    personal data is a tradable currency raises questions about
    privacy, ethics, and economic systems.

4. **Context is Key**

    Every design fiction artifact exists within a broader narrative
    context. A fictional product, for instance, is not presented in
    isolation but as part of a world with its own rules, cultures, and
    histories. This contextualization deepens engagement and invites
    audiences to explore the interconnections between different
    aspects of the imagined future.

The Process of Creating Design Fiction

The process of creating design fiction is iterative and collaborative, often
involving interdisciplinary teams of designers, technologists, writers, and
researchers. While there is no single formula, the following steps provide
a general framework:

1. **Identifying a "What If" Question**

    The process begins with a speculative question that frames the
    scope of the design fiction. For example, "What if cities were

designed exclusively for self-sustaining communities?" or "What if climate change forced humans to live underwater?"

2. **World-Building**

   Once the question is established, the next step is to build the speculative world. This involves imagining the social, cultural, technological, and economic contexts that define the future scenario. Detailed world-building ensures that the artifacts and narratives are coherent and believable.

3. **Creating Artifacts**

   Artifacts are the tangible outputs of design fiction. These can take many forms, including prototypes, posters, videos, or even fictional corporate websites. Each artifact should provide a window into the imagined world, sparking curiosity and inviting interpretation.

4. **Storytelling and Narratives**

   To connect with audiences, design fiction artifacts are often accompanied by narratives. A speculative medical device, for instance, might come with a fictional patient's testimonial or a doctor's report, grounding the artifact in a relatable story.

5. **Engagement and Reflection**

   The final step is sharing the design fiction with an audience and fostering engagement. This could involve workshops, exhibitions, or online platforms where people can interact with the artifacts, share their interpretations, and discuss the implications.

Examples of Design Fiction in Action

Design fiction has been used across industries to explore possibilities and inspire innovation. Here are a few notable examples:

1. **The Future of Self-Driving Cars**

    The automotive industry has embraced design fiction to envision the implications of autonomous vehicles. One project imagined a future where self-driving cars could be personalized as mobile offices, gyms, or even bedrooms, exploring the societal shifts that might accompany such changes.

2. **Speculative Wearable Technology**

    A design fiction project might create a fictional wearable device that monitors not only physical health but also emotional states. Through speculative advertisements and user manuals, the project could raise questions about surveillance, consent, and the commodification of emotions.

3. **Post-Apocalyptic Consumer Products**

    Speculative designers have created fictional product catalogs for a post-apocalyptic world, featuring items like portable water filters and solar-powered communication devices. These artifacts provoke reflection on resilience, resourcefulness, and the environmental challenges of the future.

The Role of Design Fiction in Social Change

One of the most powerful applications of design fiction lies in its potential to drive social change. By imagining alternative futures, design fiction can highlight systemic injustices, inspire activism, and envision equitable solutions.

For example, a design fiction project might explore a future where marginalized communities control their own technological ecosystems, challenging existing power dynamics and offering a vision of technological sovereignty. Such projects not only provoke thought but also empower communities to imagine and pursue transformative change.

Design Fiction Meets Latino Narratives

Latino design fiction represents a unique and vibrant intersection of cultural richness and speculative imagination. By drawing on Latino traditions, folklore, and lived experiences, it offers alternative perspectives on the future that challenge dominant narratives.

A Latino design fiction project might imagine a future where traditional healing practices are integrated with advanced medical technology, creating a healthcare system that values cultural knowledge alongside scientific innovation. Another project might envision a world where migration is celebrated as a source of strength, exploring the cultural hybridity that emerges in transnational communities.

By fusing design fiction with Latino narratives, these projects not only celebrate cultural heritage but also push the boundaries of what futures are possible, creating spaces for dialogue, reflection, and innovation.

Design fiction, as a discipline and a practice, holds the power to reframe our understanding of the future. By blending imagination with critical thinking, it challenges us to consider what kind of world we want to create—and what role we can play in shaping it. Through speculative artifacts, immersive narratives, and provocative questions, design fiction invites us to step into the unknown, not as passive observers but as active participants in the act of creation.

Chapter 4

Where Culture Meets Speculation

Speculation has always been a way for humanity to test the boundaries of possibility, but when it intersects with culture, it becomes something far more powerful. It becomes a way of reframing identity, preserving heritage, and imagining futures that center on voices often excluded from dominant narratives. This chapter explores how the fusion of culture and speculation—particularly through the lens of Latino narratives and design fiction—creates vibrant, transformative storytelling that reshapes our understanding of identity, history, and potential.

Cultural Foundations of Speculative Thinking

Culture is the essence of who we are—a mosaic of traditions, languages, beliefs, and practices passed through generations. It shapes how we see the world and how we imagine its possibilities. Speculation, at its core, is an imaginative process that asks "what if?" questions to envision alternate realities. When these two forces merge, they generate stories that are not only inventive but also deeply rooted in cultural experience.

In many ways, cultural traditions themselves are speculative. Myths and folklore, for example, often serve as speculative frameworks, imagining the origins of life, the nature of the divine, or the moral structures of society. In Latino cultures, stories of *La Llorona* (the weeping woman) and *El Cucuy* (the bogeyman) speculate on human behavior, morality, and the unknown. These tales function as both cautionary fables and windows into the values and fears of the communities that created them.

Speculation through culture is also a means of resilience. For communities that have faced colonization, migration, or systemic oppression, storytelling becomes a way to preserve identity and envision futures that challenge dominant paradigms. By blending traditional elements with imaginative reimaginings, cultural speculation offers an alternative narrative that celebrates heritage while pushing the boundaries of possibility.

Latino Narratives as Speculative Landscapes

Latino narratives provide fertile ground for speculative storytelling because of their inherent hybridity. The Latino experience is shaped by the convergence of multiple influences: indigenous, African, European, and, more recently, North American. This cultural richness lends itself naturally to speculative exploration, creating narratives that are as diverse as the people who tell them.

1. **The Intersection of Folklore and Futurism**

   One of the most compelling aspects of Latino speculative narratives is the blending of ancient folklore with futuristic speculation. For instance, a story might reimagine the Mayan underworld as a virtual reality space, or a modern cityscape inhabited by the spirits of Aztec deities. This fusion allows writers to honor their cultural heritage while exploring its relevance in a rapidly changing world.

A notable example is Silvia Moreno-Garcia's *Gods of Jade and Shadow*, which draws on Mayan mythology to craft a fantastical tale of a young woman's journey through the underworld. The novel bridges the past and present, creating a speculative space where ancient myths intersect with 20th-century Mexican society.

2. **Speculating on Migration and Diaspora**

Migration is a central theme in many Latino narratives, reflecting both historical realities and contemporary experiences. In speculative storytelling, migration often takes on new dimensions—crossing not only physical borders but also temporal and metaphysical ones. For example, stories might imagine migration to other planets, blending the struggle for survival with themes of cultural preservation and adaptation.

In the short story *The Book of Martha* by Octavia E. Butler, though not explicitly Latino, the themes resonate deeply with diaspora narratives: the protagonist is given the power to shape humanity's future by a godlike being. A Latino reimagining might frame this story through the lens of migration, with the protagonist wrestling with the question of how to preserve their community's cultural identity while navigating a broader societal transformation.

3. **Community as Speculative Inspiration**

Latino narratives often emphasize the importance of community, both as a source of strength and as a space for resistance. Speculative stories inspired by this theme might envision futuristic barrios where technology is designed to enhance communal living or utopian societies built on principles of mutual aid and cultural preservation.

For example, a speculative project might imagine a future where Latino communities develop their own autonomous technological ecosystems, rejecting corporate surveillance and creating systems rooted in shared cultural values. These stories challenge the individualistic ethos of much speculative fiction, offering instead a vision of collective empowerment.

Design Fiction as a Cultural Lens

Design fiction provides a unique way to explore the intersection of culture and speculation. By creating tangible artifacts and scenarios that reflect cultural experiences, it brings speculative narratives to life in ways that are immediate and impactful.

1. **Artifacts as Cultural Signifiers**

   In design fiction, artifacts are not just objects; they are carriers of meaning. A speculative artifact rooted in Latino culture might be a wearable device that translates indigenous languages in real time, preserving endangered languages while bridging generational divides. Another example could be a fictional cookbook that combines recipes with speculative stories of how food evolves in a climate-challenged future.

   These artifacts do more than speculate—they celebrate cultural heritage while imagining how it might evolve in new contexts. By grounding speculative design in cultural specificity, they create futures that are both imaginative and deeply personal.

2. **Storytelling Through Contextualization**

    Design fiction artifacts are most powerful when they are contextualized within a broader narrative. For instance, a speculative advertisement for a futuristic agricultural tool could tell the story of a rural Latino community reclaiming ancestral farming practices through advanced technology. This approach not only imagines a new artifact but also situates it within a cultural and social framework, making the speculation more relatable and thought-provoking.

Themes in Culturally-Rooted Speculation

When culture meets speculation, certain themes often emerge, reflecting the unique concerns and aspirations of the communities involved. In Latino speculative storytelling, these themes include:

1. **Hybridity and Duality**

    The blending of multiple cultural influences is a hallmark of Latino narratives, and this hybridity often finds expression in speculative stories. For example, a character might navigate two worlds—one rooted in ancestral traditions and the other in a hyper-technological future—struggling to reconcile their dual identities.

2. **Resistance and Reclamation**

    Speculative storytelling offers a space for resistance, challenging dominant narratives and reclaiming marginalized voices. In Latino narratives, this might involve reimagining colonial histories from indigenous perspectives or envisioning futures where Latino communities thrive despite systemic oppression.

3. **Environmental Stewardship**

   Many Latino communities have deep connections to the land, informed by both indigenous traditions and contemporary struggles for environmental justice. Speculative stories often reflect this relationship, imagining futures where sustainable practices and cultural knowledge play a central role in addressing ecological crises.

Case Studies in Cultural Speculation

To better understand the transformative potential of culturally-rooted speculation, it is helpful to examine specific examples that highlight the interplay between culture and imagination.

1. **Afrofuturism as a Parallel**

   While not Latino, Afrofuturism provides a valuable model for understanding how speculative storytelling can center marginalized cultural perspectives. Works like Octavia Butler's *Kindred* and Ryan Coogler's *Black Panther* use speculative frameworks to explore themes of identity, resistance, and empowerment. These stories reimagine the past and future through a distinctly African and African-American lens, offering parallels and inspiration for Latino speculative narratives.

2. **Imagining a Post-Border World**

    A speculative project might envision a future where physical and political borders have dissolved, creating a transnational society shaped by the cultural contributions of migrant communities. This scenario could explore questions of identity, belonging, and the preservation of cultural heritage in a borderless world.

3. **Reclaiming Indigenous Futures**

    Another example could involve imagining a future where indigenous knowledge systems are integrated into cutting-edge technologies, creating a harmonious balance between tradition and innovation. A story might depict a future where Mayan mathematics informs the development of advanced quantum computing, challenging the narrative of Western technological dominance.

The Transformative Power of Cultural Speculation

The fusion of culture and speculation is not just a creative exercise—it is a transformative act. By centering cultural perspectives in speculative narratives, writers and designers can challenge stereotypes, inspire new ways of thinking, and create spaces for marginalized voices to be heard. This process not only enriches the speculative genres but also redefines the possibilities of storytelling itself.

Chapter 5

Building Futures with Design Fiction

The future is not a fixed destination—it is a landscape of infinite possibilities shaped by the choices we make today. Design fiction offers a unique and dynamic approach to envisioning and crafting these futures. By blending speculative thinking with tangible artifacts and scenarios, it enables us to explore potential paths, question assumptions, and challenge societal norms. This chapter takes an in-depth look at how design fiction builds futures, focusing on its methodologies, practical applications, and transformative power.

Understanding the Foundations of Future-Building

Before delving into the mechanics of design fiction, it's important to understand its role in future-building. Unlike forecasting, which attempts to predict future trends based on current data, or utopian/dystopian storytelling, which often presents extreme visions of what could be, design fiction occupies a middle ground. It uses speculative artifacts and narratives to probe the "what ifs" of tomorrow, offering a sandbox for experimentation and dialogue.

1. **A Constructive Approach to Speculation**

    Design fiction is inherently constructive. It doesn't simply present problems; it explores potential solutions and their implications.

For example, instead of merely imagining a future where climate change has rendered cities uninhabitable, design fiction might propose speculative technologies or urban systems that help humanity adapt to such conditions.

2. **Provocation Through Tangibility**

   The power of design fiction lies in its ability to make the abstract tangible. A speculative artifact—such as a prototype of a device that translates thought into language—brings a concept to life, enabling people to engage with it in a visceral and immediate way. This tangibility not only sparks imagination but also invites critical reflection on the social, ethical, and practical implications of the imagined future.

The Process of Building Futures with Design Fiction

Creating futures through design fiction is a multi-faceted process that requires a balance of creativity, research, and critical thinking. While the specifics may vary depending on the project, the following steps provide a general framework for building futures using design fiction:

1. **Define the Purpose**

   Every design fiction project begins with a clear purpose. What question are you trying to explore? What issue are you addressing? For instance, a project might aim to envision how future generations will interact with technology or explore the cultural impact of new forms of governance.

2. **Identify the Key Drivers**

   Once the purpose is established, the next step is to identify the drivers shaping the speculative scenario. These drivers can include technological advancements, societal shifts, environmental changes, or cultural trends. For example, a speculative project on future cities might consider the effects of automation, climate migration, and the growing importance of localized economies.

3. **World-Building**

At the heart of every design fiction project is world-building. This involves creating a coherent and immersive environment in which the speculative scenario unfolds. World-building requires attention to detail, from the physical and technological aspects of the imagined world to its social, political, and cultural dimensions.

For example, if the project envisions a future where bilingual AI systems mediate cultural exchange, the world-building process might explore questions such as: What languages dominate? How do AI systems influence human relationships? What are the societal implications of universal translation?

4. **Design the Artifacts**

Artifacts are the tangible outputs of design fiction. They serve as windows into the imagined world, providing a glimpse of its technologies, practices, and values. Common types of artifacts include prototypes, advertisements, user manuals, and fictional news reports.

For instance, a speculative artifact might take the form of a "memory capsule" that allows users to store and revisit their experiences. This artifact could be accompanied by a user manual explaining its features, a customer review highlighting its emotional impact, and a marketing campaign situating it within the imagined society.

5. **Craft the Narrative**

   While artifacts are central to design fiction, they are most impactful when embedded within a narrative context. The narrative provides a framework for understanding the artifact's purpose, origins, and significance. For example, the story behind a speculative wearable device might explore how it transformed the life of a fictional user, highlighting both its benefits and unintended consequences.

6. **Engage the Audience**

   The final step is to share the design fiction with an audience and facilitate engagement. This might involve exhibiting the artifacts in a gallery, hosting a workshop to discuss their implications, or publishing the project as a multimedia story. Audience feedback is an integral part of the process, offering new perspectives and insights that can refine and expand the speculative scenario.

Applications of Design Fiction

Design fiction has found applications across a wide range of fields, from technology and urban planning to education and social justice. Its ability to bridge imagination and reality makes it a valuable tool for exploring complex challenges and generating innovative ideas.

1. **Technology and Innovation**

   In the tech industry, design fiction is often used to anticipate the implications of emerging technologies. By creating speculative prototypes and scenarios, designers and engineers can explore how new technologies might be integrated into daily life, identify potential risks, and refine their designs accordingly.

   For example, a tech company might use design fiction to imagine the future of augmented reality (AR). The project could involve creating speculative AR glasses that display personalized health data, designing user interfaces, and crafting narratives about how this technology reshapes healthcare and privacy.

2. **Urban Planning and Architecture**

   Design fiction is also a powerful tool for envisioning the future of cities and communities. It allows urban planners and architects to experiment with new ideas, test potential solutions, and engage stakeholders in conversations about the future of their environments.

   A speculative project on sustainable urban design might envision a future where cities are powered entirely by renewable energy, featuring prototypes of self-sustaining buildings, interactive public spaces, and systems for recycling water and waste. These artifacts could be presented in a fictional urban planning report, complete with interviews from "residents" of the imagined city.

3. **Education and Learning**

   In education, design fiction can be used to explore the future of teaching and learning. By imagining new methods, technologies, and environments, educators can experiment with innovative approaches to pedagogy and prepare students for the challenges of tomorrow.

For instance, a design fiction project might imagine a future classroom equipped with AI tutors, virtual reality field trips, and personalized learning pathways. Accompanying narratives could explore how these innovations impact student engagement, teacher roles, and access to education.

4. **Social Justice and Equity**

   Design fiction offers a platform for marginalized communities to envision and articulate their own futures. By centering the voices and experiences of those often excluded from mainstream narratives, design fiction can challenge systemic inequities and inspire transformative change.

   A social justice-oriented project might create speculative artifacts and scenarios imagining a world where indigenous knowledge systems inform climate policy, or where technology is designed to dismantle, rather than reinforce, social hierarchies.

Case Studies: Building Futures with Design Fiction

1. **Near Future Laboratory's "Corner Convenience"**

   In this project, the Near Future Laboratory created a series of speculative products for a fictional convenience store in the near future. The artifacts included items like a caffeinated toothpaste and a smart energy drink, each accompanied by packaging, advertisements, and narratives that situated them within the imagined world. This project explored the commercialization of convenience and its implications for consumer behavior and culture.

2. **The Extrapolation Factory**

The Extrapolation Factory specializes in participatory design fiction projects that involve community members in imagining and prototyping futures. In one project, they worked with residents of a coastal community to envision solutions for rising sea levels. The resulting artifacts, including speculative evacuation kits and floating homes, reflected the community's concerns and aspirations while sparking broader conversations about climate resilience.

3. **IKEA's "Tomorrow's Meatball"**

IKEA's Space10 lab used design fiction to explore the future of food. The project imagined alternative versions of IKEA's iconic meatballs, made from ingredients like lab-grown meat, insects, and algae. Each speculative meatball was accompanied by a story about its production, environmental impact, and cultural significance, inviting audiences to consider the future of sustainable eating.

The Impact of Design Fiction

Building futures with design fiction is not just an exercise in creativity—it is a catalyst for change. By making the abstract concrete, it allows us to confront the ethical, social, and practical implications of our choices. It challenges us to think beyond the status quo, empowering us to imagine and create futures that are inclusive, innovative, and transformative.

47

Through its unique blend of speculation, design, and storytelling, design fiction offers a powerful way to explore the complexities of the future. Whether used to anticipate the next technological breakthrough, reimagine urban life, or challenge societal norms, it provides a framework for thinking critically and creatively about the world we want to build.

Chapter 6

Case Studies in Latino Design Fiction

Latino design fiction is a burgeoning field that combines the speculative power of design fiction with the rich cultural tapestry of Latino narratives. By exploring Latino histories, traditions, and future imaginaries, these projects offer fresh perspectives on technology, identity, and resilience. This chapter dives into detailed case studies that highlight how Latino design fiction brings new voices to the speculative space, showcasing the creativity, ingenuity, and cultural specificity that define this approach.

Case Study 1: The Speculative Barrio—A Vision of Autonomous Community Design

In this project, a group of Mexican-American designers imagined a future barrio, or neighborhood, that operates as a self-sustaining ecosystem. Called *Barrio Futuro*, this speculative design fiction addressed themes of cultural preservation, environmental sustainability, and technological sovereignty.

1. **The Concept**

   Barrio Futuro envisions a neighborhood designed to resist gentrification and climate change while fostering community-led innovation. Residents of this speculative barrio create and govern

48

their own technologies, bypassing corporate systems to maintain cultural autonomy. The project integrates traditional architectural styles with futuristic green technologies, such as algae-based energy systems and biodegradable construction materials.

2. **Artifacts**

   The designers created a series of speculative artifacts, including:

   - **Solar Azulejos (Tiles):** Decorative solar panels styled after traditional Mexican ceramic tiles that generate clean energy while preserving cultural aesthetics.

   - **Community Blockchain:** A localized blockchain system allowing residents to trade resources, share skills, and store cultural archives securely.

   - **Augmented Altar:** A digital altar combining virtual reality (VR) with physical offerings, enabling families to honor ancestors while interacting with historical and genealogical data.

3. **Narrative**

   The project was presented as a fictional community planning report from the year 2042, featuring testimonials from imagined residents. Stories ranged from a grandmother who uses the Augmented Altar to teach her grandchildren about their heritage to a local entrepreneur who develops AI-powered tools tailored to the barrio's needs.

4. **Impact**

   Barrio Futuro provoked discussions about urban planning, cultural preservation, and the ethics of localized technology. It challenged the audience to imagine a future where Latino communities thrive on their own terms, blending ancestral knowledge with cutting-edge innovation.

Case Study 2: Post-Colonial Space Travel—Rethinking Migration Beyond Earth

This project, *El Otro Horizonte* (The Other Horizon), was a speculative design fiction exploring how Latino migration narratives might evolve in a future where space colonization becomes a reality. Developed by a team of Puerto Rican and Venezuelan creators, the project reimagines migration not as an escape but as an act of reclamation and cultural expansion.

1. **The Concept**

   El Otro Horizonte proposes a future where Earth's marginalized populations lead the charge in space exploration, bringing their histories and cultures into the stars. Instead of colonizing planets in the traditional sense, these migrants build floating cultural hubs that adapt to interstellar conditions while preserving Earth-bound traditions.

2. **Artifacts**

   Key speculative artifacts included:

   - **Cocina Cósmica (Cosmic Kitchen):** A portable device designed to replicate traditional cooking methods in zero gravity, enabling migrants to retain culinary traditions while living in space.

   - **Constellation Weavers:** Tools for creating textiles in

microgravity, inspired by indigenous weaving techniques, to decorate and personalize communal spaces.

- o **Memory Lanterns:** Bioluminescent orbs that store oral histories and family stories, which can be passed down through generations.

3. **Narrative**

The project was framed as a documentary from 2175, chronicling the lives of Latino spacefarers aboard *La Arca Celeste*, a modular space station orbiting Proxima Centauri. Personal vignettes included a young poet composing verses inspired by cosmic vistas and an elder weaving constellations into textiles as a map for future travelers.

4. **Impact**

El Otro Horizonte shifted the conversation about space exploration away from technological conquest to cultural preservation and adaptation. It encouraged audiences to think critically about how marginalized communities could shape interstellar futures.

Case Study 3: Healing Through Ancestral Biotechnologies

This design fiction project, *Semillas del Futuro* (Seeds of the Future), explored the fusion of ancestral agricultural practices with speculative biotechnology. Created by a multidisciplinary team of agronomists, designers, and storytellers from Colombia and Mexico, the project tackled themes of environmental justice, food security, and indigenous knowledge.

1. **The Concept**

   The project imagined a future where biotechnologies are developed collaboratively with indigenous communities to address climate challenges. These technologies emphasize harmony with nature, drawing on centuries-old agricultural wisdom.

2. **Artifacts**

   The speculative artifacts included:

   - **Living Canals:** A network of bioengineered waterways that mimic the ancient Aztec chinampas system, using living organisms to purify water and grow crops.

   - **Seed Story Capsules:** Genetically modified seeds encoded with cultural knowledge and traditional farming practices, designed to grow into plants that "teach" through visual cues and scents.

   - **Ancestral Soil Monitors:** AI-enabled tools that analyze soil health while narrating stories about its historical significance.

3. **Narrative**

   Presented as a series of "dispatches from the field" in 2090, the project followed a fictional agronomist documenting her work in a rewilded Amazon basin. Her notes detailed the challenges of implementing these technologies and the cultural exchanges that enriched the process.

4. **Impact**

   Semillas del Futuro highlighted the potential of combining modern science with ancestral knowledge, emphasizing the need for culturally respectful innovation in addressing global ecological crises.

Case Study 4: Speculative Borderlands—Reimagining Migration and Connection

In *Fronteras Invisibles* (Invisible Borders), a team of Chicano artists and technologists explored a speculative future where border regions between nations become zones of cultural fusion and innovation, rather than sites of division.

1. **The Concept**

   The project proposed an alternative vision for borderlands, imagining them as collaborative spaces governed by transnational communities rather than nation-states. These zones leverage advanced technologies to foster dialogue, creativity, and mutual support.

2. **Artifacts**

   The project included speculative artifacts like:
   - **Bilingual AI Mediators:** Devices that facilitate instant translation and cultural exchange during negotiations or communal events.
   - **Borderless Currency:** A blockchain-based economic system enabling trade and resource sharing across nations.

- ○ **Memory Walls:** Interactive installations displaying holographic stories from both sides of the border, inviting reflection and empathy.

3. **Narrative**

   The narrative unfolded as a virtual museum exhibition in 2075, showcasing the artifacts alongside fictional testimonials from individuals living in these speculative borderlands. Stories included a musician whose work drew on cross-border traditions and a teacher using AI to educate students in bilingual classrooms.

4. **Impact**

   Fronteras Invisibles sparked conversations about the role of borders in shaping identity and the potential for technology to transform spaces of division into places of connection.

Case Study 5: Speculative Health and Well-Being

Raíces Vivas (Living Roots) imagined a future where Latino communities lead a global movement toward holistic health, blending traditional healing practices with advanced medical technologies.

1. **The Concept**

   In this project, health care becomes a community-driven endeavor rooted in cultural knowledge. Traditional remedies are enhanced with biotechnology, and care systems are reimagined to prioritize prevention and holistic well-being.

2. **Artifacts**

   Artifacts included:

   - **Digital Curandero Kits:** Wearable devices programmed with AI algorithms that analyze users' health data while incorporating traditional healing advice.
   - **Botanical Clinics:** Mobile health centers designed like greenhouses, where patients receive treatments derived from genetically enhanced medicinal plants.
   - **Story Healing Pods:** Immersive VR environments that use storytelling as therapy, drawing on patients' cultural backgrounds to promote mental health.

3. **Narrative**

   The narrative followed a fictional community health worker using these tools to address public health challenges in a post-pandemic world. Her experiences highlighted the interplay between modern medicine and traditional wisdom.

4. **Impact**

   Raíces Vivas redefined health care as a culturally embedded practice, offering a speculative model for integrating science and tradition to improve well-being.

Through these case studies, we see how Latino design fiction uses speculative tools to imagine inclusive, culturally rich futures. By centering cultural identity and innovation, these projects challenge conventional narratives and inspire audiences to think differently about what is possible. These visions of the future are not only imaginative but also deeply rooted in the lived experiences and aspirations of Latino communities.

Chapter 7

Writing Your Own Speculative Stories

Writing speculative stories is an exhilarating creative exercise. It invites you to venture beyond the known, to experiment with the improbable, and to construct new worlds that challenge, reflect, and expand the boundaries of our understanding. While the prospect of crafting speculative fiction may seem daunting, it is a process that combines imagination, structure, and research. This chapter provides a comprehensive guide to writing your own speculative stories, breaking down the creative process into actionable steps while offering practical tips to help you craft narratives that captivate readers and explore profound ideas.

Understanding the Core of Speculative Storytelling

Before diving into the mechanics of writing, it's essential to understand what makes speculative storytelling unique. At its heart, speculative fiction asks, *What if?* It is a genre that thrives on possibilities—whether rooted in science, magic, mythology, or alternate history. However, speculative stories are not defined solely by their imaginative elements; they are grounded in universal themes, relatable characters, and coherent worlds.

- **The Role of the "What If" Question**

  Every speculative story begins with a single question. What if humans could communicate telepathically? What if a small town vanished overnight? What if climate change created a new species of sentient ocean creatures? These questions form the foundation of your narrative, offering a springboard for exploration and creativity.

- **Balancing the Familiar and the Strange**

  Speculative fiction is most effective when it balances the familiar with the strange. Readers need an anchor—something they recognize and relate to—amid the extraordinary. For example, a story about intergalactic refugees might echo real-world experiences of migration and displacement, providing emotional resonance in an unfamiliar setting.

Step 1: Finding Your Speculative Idea

Every great speculative story starts with an idea, but how do you find one that feels both unique and compelling? Here are some strategies to help you identify and develop your speculative premise:

1. **Observe the World Around You**

   The best speculative ideas often stem from observing current events, societal trends, and emerging technologies. Ask yourself how these might evolve over time. For instance:

   - How will artificial intelligence shape human relationships in the future?
   - What will cities look like in a world without fossil fuels?

2. **Draw from History and Mythology**

History and mythology are rich sources of speculative inspiration. Reimagine historical events with a speculative twist, or explore myths from different cultures through a modern lens. For example:

- o What if the lost city of Atlantis were a futuristic underwater society?
- o How would history have unfolded if the Aztec Empire had never fallen?

3. **Blend Genres and Concepts**

Some of the most innovative speculative stories come from combining seemingly unrelated ideas. Think about how two or more concepts might intersect. For example:

- o A murder mystery set in a virtual reality game.
- o A fantasy world where magic is tied to environmental conservation.

4. **Explore Cultural Narratives**

Drawing from your cultural background or exploring those of others can provide unique perspectives. For example:

- o A story that imagines how ancient Mayan cosmology might inform the design of a futuristic space station.

Step 2: World-Building

World-building is the backbone of speculative storytelling. It is the process of creating the physical, social, and cultural context in which your story takes place. Whether your narrative unfolds in a distant galaxy or an alternate version of Earth, effective world-building immerses readers and enhances the plausibility of your speculative elements.

1. **Establish the Rules of Your World**

    Every speculative world operates under its own rules, which must be clear and consistent. These rules dictate how technology, magic, or society functions within the story. Ask yourself:

    o   What are the physical laws of this world? Are they different from our own?

    o   How do people live, work, and interact with each other?

    o   What are the limitations or consequences of the speculative elements?

2. **Develop a Sense of Place**

    The physical environment plays a crucial role in shaping your story. Describe the geography, architecture, and atmosphere of your world. For example:

    o   Is the planet covered in endless deserts, with cities built underground to escape the heat?

    o   Does the kingdom exist on floating islands, connected by a network of aerial bridges?

3. **Create a Social and Cultural Framework**

    Societies are shaped by their histories, traditions, and values. Think about how the speculative elements of your world influence its culture:

    o   What languages, religions, or customs define this society?

    o   How does the society view progress, innovation, or

tradition?

- o Are there conflicts between different groups, and what fuels these tensions?

4. **Anchor the World in Details**

Small details make a world feel lived-in and authentic. Consider the daily lives of your characters:

- o What do they eat? What do they wear?
- o How do they communicate? What forms of entertainment do they enjoy?

Step 3: Crafting Compelling Characters

Characters are the heart of any story, including speculative fiction. While your setting and speculative elements may draw readers in, it is your characters that will keep them invested.

1. **Give Your Characters Agency**

   Your characters should drive the story forward, making choices and facing consequences. Even in a world shaped by speculative forces, they must retain their humanity—or at least some relatable quality.

2. **Develop Motivations and Conflicts**

   What does your character want, and what stands in their way? A compelling character is one whose desires and struggles are clear to the reader. For example:

   - o A scientist struggling to reconcile their groundbreaking discovery with its ethical implications.

- ○ A teenager who must choose between loyalty to their family and a chance to escape a dystopian society.

3. **Consider Character Arcs**

Strong characters evolve over the course of the story. Think about how the events of your narrative will challenge and change your protagonist:

- ○ How does the character grow as they confront the speculative elements of the world?
- ○ What do they learn about themselves, others, or their environment?

4. **Reflect Diversity and Inclusion**

Speculative fiction offers an opportunity to imagine inclusive and diverse worlds. Consider how different identities and perspectives might shape your characters and their experiences.

Step 4: Structuring Your Story

A well-structured story keeps readers engaged from beginning to end. While speculative fiction allows for creative experimentation, most narratives benefit from a clear framework.

1. **Start with a Strong Hook**

The opening of your story should grab the reader's attention and establish the speculative premise. For example:

- ○ A sudden blackout plunges a high-tech city into chaos,

revealing hidden secrets.

  - A character wakes up in a world where their memories have been erased.

2. **Build Tension Through Conflict**

   Conflict drives the plot and keeps readers turning the pages. Whether it's a battle against external forces or an internal struggle, your narrative should escalate tension as the story progresses.

3. **Balance Pacing and Detail**

   Speculative fiction often requires detailed explanations of world-building and speculative elements, but be careful not to overwhelm the reader. Balance exposition with action, and reveal details gradually.

4. **Craft a Satisfying Resolution**

   While speculative fiction often leaves some questions unanswered, your story should provide a sense of closure. Show how the characters have changed and how the speculative elements have shaped their world.

Step 5: Writing Techniques for Speculative Fiction

1. **Show, Don't Tell**

   Rather than explaining the speculative elements outright, reveal them through action, dialogue, and sensory details. For example:

   - Instead of saying, "The city was advanced," show characters interacting with the city's technology.

2. **Use Symbolism and Metaphor**

   Speculative fiction is a fertile ground for symbolism and metaphor. Use these tools to deepen the thematic resonance of your story. For example:

   - A character's journey through a crumbling labyrinth might symbolize their inner struggle.

3. **Experiment with Language and Style**

   The tone and style of your writing should reflect the speculative elements of your story. For example:

   - In a story set in a dystopian future, the language might be stark and utilitarian.

   - In a tale inspired by mythology, the prose might be lyrical and evocative.

Step 6: Revising and Refining

Writing is rewriting. Once you have completed your draft, take the time to revise and refine your work.

1. **Seek Feedback**

   Share your story with trusted readers or writing groups to gain fresh perspectives. Pay attention to their feedback on pacing, clarity, and engagement.

2. **Polish Your World-Building**

   Ensure that your world-building is consistent and coherent. Look for any gaps or contradictions in the speculative elements.

3. **Hone Your Characters**

   Revisit your characters to ensure they are well-developed and relatable. Eliminate any unnecessary characters or subplots that detract from the main narrative.

Writing speculative stories is an iterative and deeply rewarding process. By combining imaginative speculation with thoughtful structure and compelling characters, you can create narratives that transport readers to new worlds and challenge them to see their own in a different light. Through your stories, you have the power to explore not only what could be but also what should be, inspiring readers to dream, question, and act.

Chapter 8

Designing Fictional Futures

Designing fictional futures is a creative practice that combines imagination, research, and storytelling to explore possibilities beyond the constraints of the present. It is a process that allows us to envision worlds shaped by new technologies, societal shifts, and cultural evolution. Through speculative artifacts and immersive narratives, fictional futures give us a glimpse of what might be, while challenging our understanding of what is. This chapter delves into the art and science of designing fictional futures, providing insights, methodologies, and examples to inspire your journey into the speculative realm.

The Purpose of Designing Fictional Futures

Fictional futures are not about predicting what will happen but exploring what could happen. They are a tool for innovation, critique, and cultural exploration. By designing fictional futures, we can:

- **Imagine Alternatives:** Break free from the status quo and explore unconventional possibilities.
- **Highlight Consequences:** Examine the potential impacts of technological, social, and environmental changes.
- **Foster Dialogue:** Create spaces for conversation about complex

issues, encouraging diverse perspectives.

- **Inspire Innovation:** Provide a sandbox for testing ideas and sparking creative solutions.

Whether used in storytelling, design, or activism, fictional futures have the power to transform how we think about the world and our role in shaping it.

Key Elements of Fictional Futures

Designing compelling fictional futures requires careful attention to several key elements, each of which contributes to the believability and depth of the imagined world.

1. **Speculative Foundation**

   Every fictional future begins with a speculative premise—a "what if" question that serves as the foundation for the design. For example:
   - What if humanity abandoned Earth and lived entirely on floating cities in the atmosphere of Venus?
   - What if emotions could be traded as a form of currency?

2. This speculative foundation drives the design process, providing a clear focus for exploration and creativity.

3. **World-Building**

   World-building is the process of creating the physical, social, and cultural context in which your fictional future unfolds. It involves considering:

- **Environment:** What does the world look like? How has it been shaped by the speculative premise?
- **Technology:** What technologies exist, and how do they impact daily life?
- **Culture:** How do people live, interact, and express themselves?

4. A well-built world feels coherent and immersive, drawing readers or participants into the imagined reality.

5. **Artifacts and Prototypes**

   Tangible artifacts bring fictional futures to life, making abstract ideas concrete and relatable. These might include:

   - A speculative product, such as a neural interface that allows users to share memories.
   - A fictional advertisement for a utopian transportation system.
   - A prototype of a wearable device that visualizes air quality.

6. These artifacts act as windows into the future, sparking curiosity and engagement.

7. **Narrative Context**

   Every fictional future needs a story. This narrative provides a framework for understanding the world and its inhabitants, connecting the speculative elements to human experiences. For example:

   - A story about a family navigating life in a society governed by AI laws.
   - A fictional memoir of a scientist who discovers how to

grow food in zero gravity.

8. The narrative adds depth and meaning to the fictional future, making it more relatable and thought-provoking.

The Process of Designing Fictional Futures

Creating fictional futures is an iterative and collaborative process. While there is no one-size-fits-all approach, the following steps provide a roadmap for designing compelling speculative worlds.

1. **Identify the Focus Area**

   Start by selecting a focus area for your fictional future. This could be a specific technology, societal issue, or cultural theme. For example:

   o   Focus Area: Climate change adaptation.

   o   Focus Area: The future of language in a globalized world.

2. Defining your focus area helps narrow the scope of your project and ensures that your speculative future is relevant and impactful.

3. **Research and Synthesize**

   Fictional futures are grounded in research. Gather information about your focus area, including historical trends, current developments, and expert insights. For example:

   o   Research how rising sea levels are affecting coastal communities.

   o   Explore advancements in AI-driven language translation.

4. Synthesize your findings into a framework that informs your

speculative premise and world-building.

5. **Develop the Speculative Premise**

   Use your research to craft a speculative premise that drives the design. For example:

   - Speculative Premise: By 2080, coastal cities are built on floating platforms that move with the tides.

   - Speculative Premise: In the year 2150, humanity communicates using a universal neural language that replaces spoken words.

6. This premise serves as the foundation for your fictional future, guiding every aspect of the design process.

7. **Build the World**

   Construct the physical, social, and cultural dimensions of your fictional future. Consider:

   - **Geography:** How has the physical environment changed?

   - **Society:** What are the major cultural, political, and economic systems?

   - **Technology:** What tools and innovations define this future?

8. Use visual aids, such as maps or diagrams, to help conceptualize the world.

9. **Design the Artifacts**

   Create tangible artifacts that embody the speculative elements of your future. These artifacts should be detailed and plausible, inviting engagement and interpretation. For example:

   - A speculative smartphone that reads brainwaves to predict user needs.

- A fictional newspaper article reporting on a landmark event in your imagined world.

10. **Craft the Narrative**

    Embed your artifacts within a narrative that connects them to human experiences. This could take the form of:

    - A short story or vignette.

    - A multimedia presentation combining visuals, text, and audio.

    - An interactive exhibition where participants can explore the fictional future.

11. **Iterate and Refine**

    Share your fictional future with others and gather feedback. Use this input to refine your designs and narratives, ensuring that they are coherent, engaging, and thought-provoking.

Examples of Fictional Futures

To illustrate the potential of designing fictional futures, here are some examples that highlight diverse approaches and themes:

1. **Future Food Systems**

   Speculative Premise: In a world where conventional farming is no longer viable, food is grown in vertical bioreactors powered by algae.

   - Artifact: A speculative grocery store catalog showcasing bioreactor-grown products.

   - Narrative: The story of a chef adapting traditional recipes to this new form of agriculture.

2. **Post-Human Governance**

Speculative Premise: After the collapse of traditional governments, a global AI system is established to make unbiased decisions.

- o Artifact: A speculative voting interface that allows citizens to input preferences for AI analysis.
- o Narrative: A fictional debate between two citizens about the ethics of AI governance.

3. **Interstellar Migration**

Speculative Premise: Humanity establishes colonies on distant planets, creating new cultural identities.

- o Artifact: A speculative guidebook for new settlers, including survival tips and cultural etiquette.
- o Narrative: The memoir of a settler grappling with the loss of Earth and the challenges of building a new society.

Challenges and Opportunities in Designing Fictional Futures

Designing fictional futures is both exciting and challenging. It requires a balance of creativity and critical thinking, as well as sensitivity to cultural and ethical considerations.

1. **Challenges**

- o **Maintaining Plausibility:** Ensuring that your speculative elements are believable and consistent.
- o **Avoiding Clichés:** Steering clear of overused tropes and

stereotypes.

   - **Engaging Diverse Audiences:** Designing futures that resonate with people from different backgrounds and perspectives.

2. **Opportunities**

   - **Fostering Innovation:** Inspiring new ideas and solutions through speculative exploration.

   - **Encouraging Empathy:** Using fictional futures to highlight underrepresented voices and experiences.

   - **Shaping Discourse:** Influencing how people think about the future and the choices we face.

Designing fictional futures is more than a creative exercise—it is a way to explore possibilities, challenge assumptions, and inspire action. By blending imagination with research and storytelling, you can craft speculative worlds that captivate, provoke, and transform. Whether you are a writer, designer, or dreamer, the tools and techniques outlined in this chapter provide a foundation for bringing your fictional futures to life.

Chapter 9

The Impact of Speculative Narratives

Speculative narratives are more than flights of imagination; they are mirrors that reflect our realities, critiques that challenge societal norms, and blueprints that inspire change. From dystopian cautionary tales to visionary utopias, speculative storytelling offers a unique lens through which we can examine the human condition and envision alternative futures. This chapter explores the profound and multifaceted impact of speculative narratives, focusing on their ability to shape culture, inspire innovation, and foster empathy.

Speculative Narratives as Cultural Commentary

Speculative narratives have long served as a vehicle for cultural critique. By reimagining the familiar in unfamiliar contexts, these stories can expose the flaws, inequities, and contradictions in our societies.

1. **Dystopian Warnings**

   Dystopian narratives are among the most recognizable forms of speculative storytelling. They depict societies where specific trends or ideologies are taken to extremes, serving as cautionary tales about the potential consequences of our actions—or inactions.

   - **Example:** George Orwell's *1984* critiques

authoritarianism and the erosion of privacy, warning against unchecked surveillance and propaganda.

- o **Example:** Margaret Atwood's *The Handmaid's Tale* explores themes of gender oppression, shining a light on the fragility of women's rights.

2. These narratives resonate because they are grounded in the anxieties of their time, extrapolating real-world issues into stark and often unsettling futures. By presenting these scenarios, dystopian stories challenge readers to confront uncomfortable truths and consider how they might alter the course of their societies.

3. **Utopian Visions**

   While less common, utopian narratives offer an optimistic counterbalance to dystopian tales. They imagine worlds where humanity has overcome its greatest challenges, providing aspirational models for what could be achieved.

   - o **Example:** Ursula K. Le Guin's *The Dispossessed* explores themes of anarchism and cooperative living, presenting a vision of a society that prioritizes collective well-being over individual gain.

   - o **Example:** Star Trek envisions a future where humanity has transcended its divisions, working together to explore the cosmos in harmony.

4. Utopian narratives inspire hope and encourage readers to think creatively about solutions to pressing global issues. They remind us that better futures are possible and worth striving for.

The Role of Speculative Narratives in Technological Innovation

Speculative storytelling is not limited to social critique; it also plays a crucial role in shaping technological innovation. By imagining future technologies and their applications, speculative narratives often inspire real-world advancements.

1. **Science Fiction as a Catalyst for Innovation**

    Many groundbreaking technologies have been directly inspired by speculative fiction. For instance:

    o   The concept of geostationary satellites, first imagined in Arthur C. Clarke's short story *The Sentinel*, became a reality through advances in aerospace engineering.

    o   Star Trek's communicator devices inspired the development of early mobile phones, with engineers citing the show as a direct influence.

2. Speculative narratives provide a creative sandbox for exploring the possibilities of emerging technologies, pushing the boundaries of what is considered feasible.

3. **Ethical Considerations of Technological Advancements**

    Speculative stories also serve as a testing ground for the ethical implications of new technologies. By envisioning how innovations might be used—or misused—these narratives provoke critical discussions about their potential impact on society.

    o   **Example:** Isaac Asimov's *Three Laws of Robotics* introduced ethical guidelines for artificial intelligence, influencing both science fiction and real-world AI research.

- **Example:** Films like *Ex Machina* and *Black Mirror* explore the darker sides of technological dependency and human-machine interactions.

4. These narratives remind us that technology is not inherently good or bad; its value lies in how it is developed, implemented, and controlled.

Fostering Empathy Through Speculative Narratives

One of the most profound impacts of speculative storytelling is its ability to foster empathy. By placing readers in unfamiliar worlds and situations, these narratives encourage them to see through the eyes of others and consider perspectives they might not encounter in their daily lives.

1. **Exploring Marginalized Experiences**

   Speculative fiction often amplifies the voices of marginalized communities, creating space for stories that challenge dominant narratives. For example:

   - N.K. Jemisin's *The Broken Earth* trilogy weaves themes of systemic oppression, environmental disaster, and resilience through the lens of speculative fantasy.
   - Silvia Moreno-Garcia's *Mexican Gothic* reclaims the Gothic tradition to explore themes of colonialism, race, and gender from a Latino perspective.

2. These stories not only entertain but also educate, inviting readers to grapple with complex issues and recognize the humanity in others.

3. **Empathy Across Time and Space**

    Speculative narratives often transcend the boundaries of time and space, encouraging readers to empathize with characters in radically different contexts. For example:

    - In Octavia Butler's *Kindred*, the protagonist—a modern Black woman—travels back in time to experience slavery firsthand, bridging the gap between historical and contemporary experiences of racial injustice.

    - Becky Chambers' *Wayfarers* series explores the lives of diverse alien species, using their struggles and triumphs as metaphors for human identity, prejudice, and connection.

4. By immersing readers in these stories, speculative narratives help to build bridges between disparate experiences, fostering a deeper understanding of our shared humanity.

Inspiring Social and Political Change

Speculative narratives have a unique capacity to inspire activism and drive social and political change. By imagining alternative futures, these stories challenge the status quo and encourage readers to envision—and work toward—a better world.

1. **Catalyzing Activism**

    Many speculative stories have become rallying cries for social movements, inspiring readers to take action in their own lives. For example:

    - Margaret Atwood's *The Handmaid's Tale* has been used as a symbol of resistance against gender-based oppression, with protestors donning the iconic red robes at marches and demonstrations.

- o The dystopian film *V for Vendetta* popularized the Guy Fawkes mask, which has become a global symbol of resistance against authoritarianism.

2. These narratives demonstrate the power of storytelling to mobilize communities and amplify the voices of the oppressed.

3. **Reimagining Governance and Policy**

   Speculative narratives often explore alternative systems of governance, offering insights into how societies might be organized more equitably. For example:

   - o Kim Stanley Robinson's *Mars Trilogy* envisions a future where humanity establishes a new society on Mars, experimenting with alternative economic and political systems.

   - o Cory Doctorow's *Walkaway* imagines a world where people create autonomous, post-scarcity communities that reject capitalism and hierarchy.

4. These stories challenge readers to think critically about existing systems and consider bold, transformative alternatives.

Speculative Narratives and Environmental Awareness

The looming threat of climate change has made environmental storytelling a vital aspect of speculative fiction. These narratives explore the consequences of ecological collapse, as well as the innovative solutions humanity might pursue.

1. **Cli-Fi (Climate Fiction)**

   Climate fiction, or cli-fi, is a subgenre of speculative storytelling that focuses on the impacts of climate change. For example:

   - Paolo Bacigalupi's *The Windup Girl* depicts a world ravaged by bioengineering and resource scarcity, exploring the socioeconomic impacts of environmental degradation.
   - Kim Stanley Robinson's *New York 2140* imagines a partially submerged New York City, using the narrative to advocate for climate resilience and collective action.

2. By dramatizing the stakes of climate change, cli-fi inspires readers to engage with environmental issues and consider their role in combating the crisis.

3. **Imagining Sustainable Futures**

   Speculative narratives also offer visions of sustainable futures, showcasing innovative solutions to environmental challenges. For example:

   - Naomi Klein's *This Changes Everything* blends speculative elements with non-fiction to explore how humanity can transition to a post-carbon economy.
   - Movies like *Avatar* present allegories about the importance of environmental stewardship and the interconnectedness of ecosystems.

4. These stories remind us that the future is not set in stone—it is shaped by the choices we make today.

Cultural Representation in Speculative Narratives

Diverse speculative narratives are essential for creating inclusive futures. By centering underrepresented voices and perspectives, these stories enrich the genre and challenge hegemonic worldviews.

1. **Reclaiming Narratives**

   Many speculative stories reimagine historical and cultural narratives, offering alternative perspectives on familiar themes. For example:

   - Rebecca Roanhorse's *Trail of Lightning* blends Navajo mythology with speculative fantasy, reclaiming indigenous stories for a modern audience.

   - Victor LaValle's *The Ballad of Black Tom* reinterprets H.P. Lovecraft's racist narratives through the lens of African-American experience.

2. These narratives empower marginalized communities to tell their own stories and assert their place in speculative worlds.

3. **Expanding the Imaginative Horizon**

   Diverse speculative narratives challenge readers to think beyond their own experiences, expanding the boundaries of what is possible. For example:

   - Aliette de Bodard's *Xuya Universe* imagines an alternate history where Asian and Mesoamerican cultures dominate space exploration, offering a fresh perspective on humanity's future.

   - Nnedi Okorafor's *Binti* series combines African cultural elements with science fiction, exploring themes of identity, belonging, and resilience.

4. These stories enrich the speculative genre, ensuring that it reflects the full spectrum of human experience.

Speculative narratives are powerful tools for reflection, innovation, and transformation. By imagining alternative realities, they help us better understand our own, offering insights into the challenges we face and the possibilities we can create. Through their ability to critique, inspire, and connect, speculative stories shape not only our imagination but also our collective future.

Chapter 10

Looking Ahead The Future of Storytelling and Design

Storytelling and design have always been integral to human culture, shaping how we understand our world and imagine new possibilities. As technologies evolve and societal paradigms shift, the ways we tell stories and create designs are undergoing profound transformations. This chapter explores the future of storytelling and design, examining emerging trends, the integration of technology and creativity, and the potential for both fields to inspire meaningful change.

The Convergence of Storytelling and Design

Traditionally, storytelling and design have been viewed as distinct disciplines. Storytelling communicates ideas and emotions through narrative, while design focuses on solving problems and creating functional systems. However, the boundaries between these fields are increasingly blurred. Modern storytelling often relies on design elements to create immersive experiences, while design frequently incorporates narrative to communicate purpose and context.

1. Narrative-Driven Design

The integration of storytelling into design is reshaping how products, systems, and experiences are created. Designers are using narrative to:

- **Humanize Technology:** By embedding stories in user interfaces, designers make technology more relatable and intuitive. For instance, smart home devices like Alexa and Google Assistant use conversational narratives to create a sense of companionship.
- **Communicate Purpose:** Narrative frameworks help users understand the purpose and functionality of a design. For example, a fitness app might use a gamified storyline to encourage consistent use.

2. **Design-Driven Storytelling**

Conversely, design elements are transforming storytelling by enhancing the way narratives are presented and experienced. From interactive storytelling platforms to visually stunning graphic novels, design is central to crafting compelling stories. Examples include:

- **Virtual Reality (VR):** Immersive VR experiences allow audiences to step inside a story, experiencing it as active participants rather than passive observers.
- **Augmented Reality (AR):** AR adds layers of narrative to physical spaces, such as interactive museum exhibits or location-based games like *Pokémon GO*.

Emerging Trends in Storytelling

The future of storytelling is being shaped by technological advancements, evolving audience expectations, and a growing emphasis on inclusivity and innovation. Here are some of the most significant trends shaping the future of narrative:

1. **Immersive Storytelling**

   Technologies like VR, AR, and mixed reality (MR) are redefining how stories are told and experienced. These platforms create multisensory environments that engage audiences on a deeper level.

   - **Examples:**
     - VR experiences like *Wolves in the Walls* bring Neil Gaiman's stories to life through immersive environments.
     - AR-enhanced books like *Between Page and Screen* blend physical and digital storytelling.

Immersive storytelling not only entertains but also fosters empathy by allowing audiences to experience narratives from different perspectives.

2. **Interactive and Participatory Narratives**

   Interactivity is becoming a hallmark of modern storytelling. Audiences increasingly expect to play a role in shaping the story, whether through choices, contributions, or real-time interactions.

   - **Examples:**
     - Netflix's *Bandersnatch* allows viewers to make decisions that influence the plot's outcome.
     - Community-driven storytelling platforms like *Wattpad* enable readers to contribute ideas and vote on plot directions.

These participatory narratives create a sense of agency and investment, transforming audiences into co-creators.

3. **AI-Generated Stories**

   Advances in artificial intelligence (AI) are enabling new forms of storytelling. AI algorithms can generate narratives, create dialogue, and even compose music for stories.

   - **Examples:**
     - AI-driven platforms like *Sudowrite* assist writers by generating plot ideas and refining prose.
     - Video games like *AI Dungeon* use machine learning to create adaptive, player-driven narratives.

While AI-generated stories are still in their infancy, they raise intriguing questions about authorship, creativity, and the nature of storytelling.

4. **Serialized and Episodic Content**

   Serialized storytelling, long popular in television and literature, is gaining traction in digital formats. Episodic content allows creators to build anticipation and deepen audience engagement over time.

   - **Examples:**
     - Podcast dramas like *Welcome to Night Vale* build immersive worlds through episodic narratives.
     - Serialized fiction platforms like *Radish* deliver bite-sized stories tailored for mobile audiences.

Emerging Trends in Design

Design, like storytelling, is evolving in response to technological, cultural, and environmental changes. The future of design is characterized by innovation, sustainability, and inclusivity.

1. **Human-Centered Design**

   Human-centered design focuses on creating products and systems that prioritize the needs, desires, and experiences of users. This approach is becoming increasingly important as technologies grow more complex.

   - **Examples:**
     - Wearable devices like the Apple Watch are designed to integrate seamlessly into daily life while addressing specific health and lifestyle needs.
     - Educational platforms like Duolingo use gamified design to make language learning accessible and enjoyable.

By centering the user, designers can create solutions that are not only functional but also meaningful.

2. **Sustainable and Regenerative Design**

   As environmental concerns grow, designers are moving beyond sustainability toward regenerative practices that actively restore ecosystems and communities.

   - **Examples:**
     - Circular design principles are being applied to

create products with minimal waste, such as modular furniture that can be easily repaired and repurposed.

- ■ Regenerative architecture, like Bosco Verticale in Milan, integrates vegetation into urban buildings to improve air quality and biodiversity.

These practices reflect a shift toward design that benefits both people and the planet.

3. **Speculative Design**

   Speculative design explores hypothetical futures, using artifacts and scenarios to provoke thought and spark innovation.

   o **Examples:**

     - ■ Dunne & Raby's *United Micro Kingdoms* imagines four alternative societal structures, each governed by a different ideology.
     - ■ IKEA's *Future Living Lab* creates speculative furniture concepts to envision how people might live in the future.

Speculative design challenges conventional assumptions and inspires new ways of thinking about the future.

4. **Inclusive and Accessible Design**

   The future of design is increasingly focused on inclusivity, ensuring that products and systems are accessible to diverse populations.

   o **Examples:**

- Microsoft's Inclusive Design Toolkit helps designers create technology that accommodates a range of abilities.
- Adaptive clothing lines like Tommy Hilfiger's *Adaptive Collection* provide fashionable options for people with disabilities.

Inclusive design reflects a commitment to equity, empowering individuals and communities to participate fully in society.

The Role of Artificial Intelligence in Storytelling and Design

AI is poised to play a transformative role in both storytelling and design, enabling new possibilities while raising ethical and creative questions.

1. **AI as a Creative Partner**

   AI tools are increasingly being used to assist creators in generating ideas, automating tasks, and enhancing workflows.
   - **Examples:**
     - Adobe's AI-powered tools streamline graphic design and photo editing.
     - GPT-4-based platforms assist writers by generating compelling dialogue and story arcs.

While AI can augment human creativity, it also challenges traditional notions of authorship and originality.

2. **Ethical Considerations**

   The integration of AI into storytelling and design raises important ethical questions:

   - How do we ensure that AI-generated content reflects diverse perspectives and avoids bias?
   - What role should transparency play in disclosing the use of AI in creative processes?

Addressing these questions is essential to harnessing the potential of AI responsibly.

The Intersection of Storytelling, Design, and Social Impact

Storytelling and design have always been powerful tools for social change. In the future, their combined potential will be even more critical in addressing global challenges.

1. **Amplifying Marginalized Voices**

   Inclusive storytelling and design practices can amplify underrepresented voices, fostering empathy and understanding.

   - **Examples:**
     - Storytelling initiatives like *The Moth* give individuals a platform to share personal experiences.
     - Co-design projects involve marginalized communities in the creation of solutions that reflect their needs and aspirations.

2. **Advancing Environmental Awareness**

Narrative-driven design can raise awareness about environmental issues and inspire sustainable behaviors.

- o **Examples:**
  - Interactive exhibits like *Museum of Ice Cream* use immersive storytelling to engage audiences with climate themes.
  - Documentaries like *2040* combine narrative and speculative design to envision sustainable futures.

3. **Empowering Communities**

Storytelling and design can empower communities to imagine and build their own futures.

- o **Examples:**
  - Participatory design workshops enable communities to co-create solutions for local challenges.

  - Grassroots storytelling projects document and preserve cultural heritage, ensuring that diverse histories are not lost.

The future of storytelling and design is a dynamic interplay of creativity, technology, and social innovation. By embracing these evolving practices, we can craft narratives and systems that inspire, challenge, and transform. Together, storytelling and design have the power to reimagine our world—and shape a better tomorrow.

Appendices

The appendices serve as a valuable companion to the main content of this book, offering additional resources, practical tools, and expanded insights to deepen your understanding of speculative storytelling and design fiction. Here, you will find a glossary of essential terms, suggested resources for further exploration, practical exercises to enhance your craft, and a curated list of case studies to inspire your work. Each section is designed to provide a richer, more comprehensive foundation for your journey into speculative storytelling and design.

Appendix A: Glossary of Key Terms

To navigate the interdisciplinary landscape of speculative storytelling and design fiction, a strong grasp of its terminology is essential. This glossary defines key concepts used throughout the book, providing clarity and a shared vocabulary.

1. **Artifact**

    A tangible or digital object created to represent or evoke a fictional future. Examples include prototypes, fictional advertisements, or speculative products.

2. **Cli-Fi (Climate Fiction)**

    A subgenre of speculative fiction that explores the impacts of climate change on society, ecosystems, and the future.

3. **Design Fiction**

    A creative practice that uses speculative scenarios and artifacts to explore possible futures, provoke thought, and inspire innovation.

4. **Dystopia**

A narrative depicting a society characterized by oppression, suffering, or extreme inequities, often as a cautionary tale.

5. **Futurism**

The study and practice of anticipating and exploring possible futures, often through speculative storytelling and design.

6. **Immersive Storytelling**

A narrative approach that uses technologies like VR and AR to create fully immersive experiences for the audience.

7. **Speculative Fiction**

A broad genre encompassing narratives that imagine alternate realities, including science fiction, fantasy, and alternate history.

8. **Utopia**

A narrative that envisions an idealized or perfect society, often as a critique of existing conditions or an aspirational model.

Appendix B: Resources for Further Exploration

Whether you are a seasoned writer or a curious beginner, these resources will deepen your understanding of speculative storytelling and design fiction.

1. **Books**
   - *The Left Hand of Darkness* by Ursula K. Le Guin: A masterclass in speculative world-building and exploring

gender and culture through fiction.

- *Design Fiction: A Short Essay on Design, Science, Fact, and Fiction* by Julian Bleecker: A foundational text that defines and contextualizes design fiction.

- *Sapiens: A Brief History of Humankind* by Yuval Noah Harari: While not speculative fiction, this book explores human imagination as a driving force in shaping societies.

2. **Websites and Blogs**

   - **Near Future Laboratory**: A hub for exploring cutting-edge design fiction projects and methodologies.

   - **Worldbuilding Stack Exchange**: An online community for discussing and refining world-building techniques.

3. **Courses and Workshops**

   - **Coursera: Science Fiction and Fantasy Writing**: A course designed to help writers develop speculative narratives.

   - **Speculative Futures Meetup Groups**: Local and online gatherings focused on speculative design and futures thinking.

4. **Media**

   - **Films:** *Black Mirror* (Netflix): A series of standalone stories exploring the dark sides of technology.

   - **Podcasts:** *Imaginary Worlds*: A podcast about the craft and impact of speculative storytelling.

Appendix C: Practical Exercises for Speculative Storytelling and Design

To develop your skills, it's crucial to practice. The following exercises are designed to stimulate creativity and deepen your engagement with speculative narratives and design fiction.

- **The "What If" Generator**
    - Write down five societal trends (e.g., urbanization, automation, climate change).
    - For each trend, pose a "what if" question (e.g., "What if cities were entirely underground?").
    - Choose one question and expand it into a short speculative scenario.
- **Artifact Creation**
    - Choose a speculative premise (e.g., "What if emotions could be transferred between people?").
    - Design an artifact that represents this future, such as a fictional device, a manual, or a product advertisement.
    - Write a description of how this artifact fits into the imagined world.
- **Cultural Mash-Up**
    - Select two distinct cultural traditions (e.g., Japanese tea ceremonies and Aztec rituals).
    - Imagine a speculative future where these traditions have merged.
    - Write a scene or create an artifact that reflects this fusion.

- **Reverse Engineering a Future**
  - Think of a speculative future scenario (e.g., a world without fossil fuels).
  - Work backward to imagine the steps that led to this future, including technological, social, and political changes.
  - Write a timeline or create a fictional historical artifact from this process.

Appendix D: Expanded Case Studies

Building on the case studies discussed in Chapter 6, this section provides additional examples of speculative storytelling and design fiction that push creative boundaries and inspire innovation.

1. **Hyperloop Diaries: Stories of High-Speed Futures**
   - Speculative Premise: In a future where high-speed transport connects every major city, individuals from different cultures interact daily in new and unexpected ways.
   - Artifacts: A fictional travel guide for Hyperloop passengers, detailing the cultural norms of global "transit cities."
   - Narrative: A short story about a musician who gains worldwide fame by performing in Hyperloop stations.

2. **The Digital Bazaar: A Future of Decentralized Commerce**
   - Speculative Premise: In 2050, global trade is conducted through decentralized blockchain marketplaces controlled by local communities.
   - Artifacts: A speculative cryptocurrency wallet designed to prioritize ethical sourcing and environmental sustainability.
   - Narrative: A fictional interview with a digital nomad who thrives in this new economic system.

Appendix E: Common Pitfalls and How to Avoid Them

While creating speculative narratives and design fiction, it's easy to fall into certain traps. This section identifies common pitfalls and offers strategies to overcome them.

1. **Overloading with Exposition**
   - **The Problem:** Too much background information can overwhelm readers and slow the narrative.
   - **Solution:** Show the speculative elements through action and dialogue rather than lengthy descriptions.
2. **Ignoring Human Elements**
   - **The Problem:** A focus on world-building at the expense of character development can make stories feel hollow.
   - **Solution:** Ground your speculative world in relatable human experiences and emotions.

3. **Unclear Internal Logic**

    o   **The Problem:** Inconsistent or poorly defined rules can break the immersion of your speculative world.

    o   **Solution:** Define the rules of your world early and ensure they remain consistent throughout the narrative.

4. **Relying on Clichés**

    o   **The Problem:** Overused tropes can make your story feel derivative.

    o   **Solution:** Subvert expectations by adding unique twists to familiar concepts.

Appendix F: Looking to the Future

The field of speculative storytelling and design fiction is dynamic and ever-evolving. Emerging technologies like AI, quantum computing, and brain-computer interfaces will undoubtedly reshape how we imagine and create fictional futures. Additionally, as global challenges like climate change and social inequities demand innovative solutions, speculative narratives will play a critical role in envisioning and inspiring change.

By staying curious, embracing interdisciplinary approaches, and fostering a spirit of experimentation, you can contribute to the ongoing evolution of this exciting field. These appendices provide the tools and inspiration to help you on this journey, empowering you to craft narratives and designs that challenge, provoke, and transform.

Further Reading

The landscape of speculative storytelling and design fiction is vast and constantly evolving, shaped by a wide array of thinkers, creators, and practitioners. To deepen your understanding and broaden your horizons, this curated list of books, articles, films, and other resources offers a comprehensive guide to further exploration. From foundational works to cutting-edge perspectives, these recommendations provide a roadmap for engaging with the themes, techniques, and possibilities that define this field.

Books: Foundations of Speculative Storytelling and Design

1. **Fictional Futures and Speculative Histories** by Richard Barbrook

   Barbrook's book examines the cultural and political implications of speculative storytelling. Focusing on how narratives shape societal expectations, it's an essential read for understanding the influence of speculative fiction on our collective imagination.

2. **The Dispossessed** by Ursula K. Le Guin

   A cornerstone of speculative literature, Le Guin's novel explores themes of utopia, dystopia, and anarchism through the lens of two contrasting worlds. It's a masterclass in speculative world-building and social critique.

3. **Designing for the Digital Age** by Kim Goodwin

   While not exclusively about speculative design, Goodwin's guide provides practical insights into user-centered design, a skillset that is essential for crafting believable and engaging design fiction artifacts.

4. **Radical Technologies** by Adam Greenfield

   This book examines the impact of emerging technologies such as artificial intelligence, blockchain, and augmented reality. Greenfield's critical analysis offers valuable insights for those interested in crafting speculative futures that engage with real-world technological trends.

5. **Burning Chrome** by William Gibson

   A collection of short stories that introduced many of the ideas that later became central to the cyberpunk genre. Gibson's work is a blueprint for imagining near-future speculative worlds shaped by technology.

Academic Articles and Essays

1. **"Design Fiction: A Short Essay on Design, Science, Fact, and Fiction"** by Julian Bleecker

   This foundational essay defines design fiction and explores its role in speculative practice. Bleecker's insights are indispensable for anyone interested in combining storytelling and design to envision futures.

2. **"Speculative Everything: Design, Fiction, and Social Dreaming"** by Anthony Dunne and Fiona Raby

   This essay, which complements their book of the same name, introduces speculative design as a tool for challenging assumptions and imagining alternative futures. It's a must-read for designers and futurists.

3. **"The Role of Fiction in Shaping Futures"** by Amy Chambers

   Published in *Futures Journal*, this article discusses the intersection of speculative storytelling and future studies, emphasizing the role of narratives in shaping societal attitudes and expectations.

Films and Television: Visualizing Speculative Futures

1. **Blade Runner (1982)** and **Blade Runner 2049 (2017)**

   These iconic films explore themes of artificial intelligence, environmental collapse, and identity in visually stunning speculative worlds. They serve as an excellent case study in using design elements to create immersive futures.

2. **Black Mirror (Netflix)**

   This anthology series offers a dark and thought-provoking exploration of technology's potential to shape society. Each episode is a standalone speculative narrative, making it a rich source of inspiration for those interested in short-form storytelling.

3. **Her (2013)**

   Spike Jonze's film about a man who falls in love with an AI assistant explores themes of connection, isolation, and the ethics of artificial intelligence. It's a poignant example of speculative storytelling grounded in human emotion.

4. **Arrival (2016)**

   Based on Ted Chiang's short story, *Story of Your Life*, this film combines speculative linguistics with first-contact science fiction, offering a deeply philosophical take on communication and understanding.

5. **The Man in the High Castle (Amazon Prime)**

    Adapted from Philip K. Dick's novel, this series imagines an alternate history where the Axis powers won World War II. It's a compelling example of speculative storytelling that blends history with fiction.

Graphic Novels and Comics: Visual Speculative Storytelling

1. **Saga** by Brian K. Vaughan and Fiona Staples

    This epic space opera blends science fiction and fantasy to explore themes of family, war, and love. The rich world-building and character development make it a standout in speculative visual storytelling.

2. **Watchmen** by Alan Moore and Dave Gibbons

    A deconstruction of the superhero genre, *Watchmen* combines alternate history with political critique, offering a masterclass in narrative complexity and thematic depth.

3. **The Incal** by Alejandro Jodorowsky and Moebius

    This graphic novel series is a visually stunning exploration of metaphysical and futuristic themes, making it a cornerstone of speculative comics.

Interactive Media: Participatory Speculative Storytelling

1. **Detroit: Become Human (Video Game)**

    This narrative-driven game explores themes of artificial intelligence, free will, and societal inequality through a branching storyline shaped by player choices. It's an excellent example of participatory speculative storytelling.

2. **The Stanley Parable (Video Game)**

   This interactive story challenges traditional narrative structures, using humor and existential themes to explore the nature of choice and free will.

3. **World Without Oil (Alternate Reality Game)**

   This collaborative storytelling project imagines a future energy crisis, engaging participants in crafting narratives and solutions. It's a powerful example of using speculative storytelling for activism and education.

Podcasts and Audio Dramas

1. **Imaginary Worlds**

   Hosted by Eric Molinsky, this podcast delves into the creative processes behind speculative worlds in literature, film, and other media. It's an invaluable resource for aspiring storytellers and designers.

2. **The Truth**

   This audio drama series features immersive, short-form speculative stories that explore a wide range of themes, from futuristic technology to supernatural phenomena.

3. **LeVar Burton Reads**

   LeVar Burton brings speculative short stories to life in this podcast, providing both entertainment and insights into the craft of storytelling.

Online Communities and Platforms

1. **Speculative Futures Meetup**

    A global network of local groups focused on speculative design and futures thinking. These meetups provide opportunities to connect with like-minded individuals and share ideas.

2. **Worldbuilding Stack Exchange**

    A Q&A platform where writers, designers, and enthusiasts discuss the intricacies of world-building, offering practical advice and inspiration.

3. **Wattpad**

    An online platform for serialized storytelling, Wattpad is home to a thriving community of speculative fiction writers and readers.

Journals and Periodicals

1. **Futures**

    An academic journal dedicated to future studies and speculative thinking. Articles often explore the intersection of storytelling, design, and societal change.

2. **Clarkesworld Magazine**

    A leading publisher of speculative short stories, *Clarkesworld* showcases cutting-edge science fiction and fantasy from emerging and established authors.

3. **Tor.com**

    A hub for speculative fiction enthusiasts, Tor.com features stories, essays, and commentary on a wide range of topics within the genre.

Workshops and Conferences

1. **Future of Storytelling (FoST)**

   This annual conference brings together creators, technologists, and innovators to explore the cutting edge of storytelling. Workshops and talks cover topics like VR, AI, and participatory narratives.

2. **Speculative Futures Summit**

   Focused on speculative design and futures thinking, this conference offers a platform for sharing ideas and showcasing projects.

3. **Clarion Science Fiction and Fantasy Writers' Workshop**

   A prestigious workshop for aspiring speculative fiction writers, Clarion provides mentorship from established authors and a supportive environment for developing craft.

The resources listed here represent just a fraction of the expansive world of speculative storytelling and design fiction. By engaging with these materials, you will gain fresh perspectives, refine your skills, and find inspiration for your own creative endeavors. The future is a canvas waiting to be imagined, and these tools will help you paint it with boldness, clarity, and depth.